The Worst
Day of Our Lives

The Worst Day of Our Lives

Written by
Narinder Dhami

Illustrated by
Ash Roy

Collins

Contents

Family trees

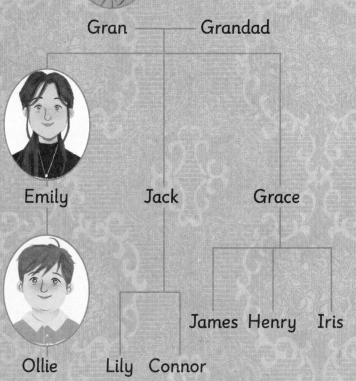

Gran ——— Grandad

Emily   Jack   Grace

Ollie   Lily Connor   James Henry   Iris

Gran ———— Grandad

Akshay

Deepa

Chapter 1

"This could be the worst day of my life," Ollie muttered.

"What did you say, sweetie?" his mum asked. She was sitting up in bed, drinking a cup of tea. A glittering white wedding dress with a matching veil hung on the back of the door.

"Oh, nothing," Ollie said quickly.

He didn't want to upset his mum, not on her wedding day. She was marrying Akshay, and he would be Ollie's new stepfather. Ollie really loved Akshay. He was kind and funny, and he was always up for a kick-around with Ollie.

No, Akshay wasn't the problem at all. It was Akshay's daughter, Deepa …

"Looks like it's going to be a lovely day, too," Mum said happily. "You really should go and have your shower now, Ollie, before everyone else wakes up."

Ollie nodded and headed for the door.
The house was packed with wedding guests
who had stayed overnight, ready for
the big day.

"And tell Deepa to do the same," his mum
called after him.

Ollie gritted his teeth.

He didn't speak to Deepa if he could help it.
No one understood how strange it felt to
have a stepsister after eight years of being
an only child.

Ollie thought it wouldn't have been *quite* so
bad if Deepa had been younger than him.
But no, they were both the same age.
Deepa was three months older than
Ollie though.

She was four centimetres taller than he was, too.

And, boy, does she go on about it, Ollie thought bitterly.

He turned the corner of the landing and cannoned straight into Deepa.

Deepa was in her dressing-gown, and her hair was wet. She'd obviously already had her shower. Ollie rolled his eyes. Typical Deepa, always one move ahead of everyone else. He went to side-step her and go into the bathroom, but Deepa blocked his path.

"I want to talk to you," she said seriously.

Ollie stared at her in complete shock. "Why?" he spluttered. He knew Deepa disliked him as much as he disliked her.

"It's about the wedding." Deepa leant against the door frame and folded her arms. "We want our parents to have a fabulous day, don't we?"

"Yes," Ollie agreed cautiously.

"So, I think we should pretend to be friends today," Deepa went on. "Just for the wedding. What do you think?"

"Well – " Ollie still felt a little wary. Was this some kind of trap? "I suppose I can manage that."

Deepa grinned. "We can always go back to not liking each other afterwards."

"Yep," Ollie said a bit too eagerly. Deepa scowled. She flounced past Ollie and knocked him slightly with her elbow on purpose.

"OW!" Ollie gasped dramatically, although it hadn't really hurt at all.

Ollie glared at Deepa's back as she walked down the landing to her bedroom. Honestly, she was SO annoying! Ollie just didn't trust Deepa one little bit …

11

A garden wedding

candy
floss

PHOTOS

13

Chapter 2

Deepa wandered downstairs to grab some breakfast. Everyone in the house was now beginning to wake up. Deepa felt very shy because she hardly knew any of the wedding guests except Ollie's gran. And Ollie seemed to have a million cousins. Her dad wasn't there, either. He'd spent the night at his best man's house.

Deepa was relieved the kitchen was empty. The wedding cake had been delivered, and she walked towards the table to admire it.

There were four layers of gold and white icing with delicate sugar flowers and tiny models of a bride and groom on the top layer.

Deepa sighed. She loved Emily, Ollie's mum,
but honestly, Ollie was just SO annoying!
This really was the worst day of her life ...

The door was nudged open.
Sausage lolloped in, his tail wagging.

"Hello, boy." Deepa stroked
the greyhound's head. She'd never been
very keen on dogs. However, Sausage had
won her over. He was Ollie's dog, though,
so Deepa ignored Sausage when Ollie
was around.

Sausage's wagging tail whacked against
the table leg, and the wedding cake
wobbled slightly.

"Out, Sausage!" Deepa said sternly.
She caught hold of the dog's collar and
took him out into the back garden. Then she
went back inside to get some cereal. It was
already a warm, sunny day. There was a bell
tent on the lawn for the wedding reception.
People were laying the tables and arranging
the flowers.

Meanwhile, Ollie dried off after his shower and slipped on jeans and a T-shirt. It was too early to dress up in his wedding outfit yet. Ollie pulled a face in the mirror. His mum wanted him to wear a suit, a waistcoat *and* a bow tie. He was NOT looking forward to it.

Ollie decided to go downstairs for breakfast. As he walked along the landing, he noticed a sheet of paper on the floor.

That's Deepa's handwriting, Ollie thought. He was curious because he could see his own name at the top of the sheet. Ollie seized the paper and examined it carefully.

Eight things I hate about Ollie!

1. His voice

2. His laugh

3. The way he walks

4. He's obsessed with FOOTBALL

5. He steals all the peanut butter cookies

6. His bedroom is always messy

7. His trainers stink

8. He tries to copy my homework

Ollie felt himself seethe with fury. He could hardly breathe. How dare Deepa write down all these things about him? They weren't true either! Well, maybe a few of them were … He *was* obsessed with football, and his bedroom *was* always messy, and maybe his trainers *did* smell, just a bit. But Deepa had no right to be so totally rude about him!

Ollie, choked with rage, headed for the stairs. He'd had enough of Deepa, and he was going to find her and tell her so!

Ollie vs. Deepa

Deepa – best arm-wrestler

Checkmate!

Deepa – best chess player

Ollie – star gamer

Deepa – fastest runner

Ollie – best baker

Ollie – best dancer

Chapter 3

Deepa was finishing her bowl of cereal when Ollie burst into the kitchen.

"Why are you charging around like an angry rhino?" Deepa asked, smirking.

"Because I just found this!" Ollie rushed furiously towards her and slapped the sheet of paper down on the kitchen worktop.

Deepa put her empty bowl down and stared curiously at the paper. Then she gasped and clapped a hand to her mouth in horror.

Ollie glared at her. "How come you can only think of eight things you hate about me?" he jeered. "I can think of *millions* of things I hate about *you*!"

"Where did you find this?"
Deepa demanded angrily. "Have you been snooping around my bedroom, Ollie?"

"No, I have NOT!" Ollie was in a real temper by now and stamped his foot. "I found it on the landing!"

Deepa chewed her lip. Secretly, she felt sick with guilt. She'd written the list as a joke with her best friend Meena. Meena had come for a sleepover, and Ollie had been annoying the two girls. The list had been their revenge. It was a mean thing to do, Deepa told herself. But she'd never meant for Ollie to see it. Why hadn't she just torn it up and thrown it away?

28

Ollie was still furious. "I'm going to show
this list to your dad," he declared.

"No, don't." Deepa began to panic. Her dad
would *not* be impressed with her. "You'll ruin
our parents' wedding – "

"Not *today*," Ollie snapped impatiently.
"I'll keep it and show it to him later."

He made a grab for the sheet of paper lying on the worktop, but Deepa seized it first.

"Give me that!" Ollie howled.

"No, it belongs to me!" Deepa held the paper high above her head out of Ollie's reach. Ollie began leaping up and down, trying to grab it. But Deepa was just too tall for him.

As Deepa backed towards the kitchen door, still holding the sheet of paper, Ollie made a superhuman effort. He launched himself at her and managed to grab a corner of it. Deepa was caught off-balance.

She stumbled and fell into the table.
Their flailing arms hit the top layer of
the wedding cake, knocking it sideways.
The top of the cake collapsed in a shower
of icing and sponge, and the tiny models of
the bride and groom fell to the floor.

Deepa and Ollie froze on the spot.
They both stared down at their arms, which
were speckled with sponge, icing and sugar.

"Look what you've done!" Deepa gasped.
"The cake is *ruined*!"

"This is all your fault!" Ollie accused her.

Ollie bent down and picked up the models of the bride and groom. The bride was still whole, but the groom was now in five pieces.

"What are we going to do?" Deepa groaned. "This is a nightmare!"

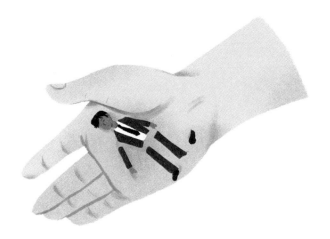

A history of wedding cakes

Ancient Greeks – a spicy wedding pie.
The pie crust wasn't eaten – just the filling!

Ancient Romans – a wedding cake of wheat
or barley. The bread was broken above
the bride's head! The bride, groom and
guests then ate the crumbs.

England 1300s–1400s – lots of small pies stacked very high. The pies were said to last for five years!

1500s–1600s – Bride pies, sometimes with live ingredients like birds or a snake!

1700s – Fruitcakes became popular.

1840s – Queen Victoria's wedding cake weighed 136 kilograms!

Chapter 4

"We can try to stick the groom back together," Ollie suggested.

"But look at the cake!" Deepa wailed.

There were lumps of icing, crumbs of cake and broken sugar flowers scattered across the table.

"You put the top layer of the cake back," Ollie said. "I'll sort the groom out!"

Ollie hurtled out of the kitchen at top speed.

Deepa was so panic-stricken, she could hardly breathe. This was a fiasco! And the wedding was only a few hours away! Carefully, she collected up the pieces of cake.

Deepa moulded the broken layer of the cake together and positioned it back on top. Then she arranged the broken icing over it as best as she could.

As Deepa replaced the bride on the cake, Ollie dashed in. He was waving a tube of PVA glue.

"Sorry I was so long," he panted. "I couldn't find the glue. We'd better be quick. Everyone's up, and guests will be coming into the kitchen for breakfast very soon."

"What do you think?" Looking worried, Deepa pointed to the cake.

Ollie frowned. "It's kind of lopsided," he replied.

"That's because some of the cake fell on the floor," Deepa snapped. "I couldn't use *that*, could I?"

"No," Ollie agreed. "It's a shame all
the flowers got smashed. They would have
helped to hide it."

"You've just given me a brilliant idea!"
Deepa declared. She sprinted out of
the kitchen and up the stairs.

Meanwhile, Ollie tried to repair the model
of the groom. He quickly became
frustrated though. The pieces just wouldn't
stick together.

"Lucky I'm a genius and I have
a back-up plan!" Ollie said to himself.
He took a tiny model from his pocket and
placed it on the cake next to the bride.

Next moment, Deepa dashed back in.
She held a packet of something in her hand.

"About those sugar flowers – " Deepa
began, but then she stopped abruptly.
"What's that on the cake?"

"It's a model from my fantasy game, *Treasure Forest*," Ollie explained.

Deepa peered at the model. "But it's a *goblin*!" she pointed out.

Ollie shrugged. "No one will notice," he insisted. "What were you saying about the flowers?"

Deepa held up the packet she was carrying. "Look, we can make some more and stick them all over the top of the cake," she said.

"*Clay* flowers?" Ollie's eyes opened wide. "What if a guest eats one by mistake?"

"We'll just have to stand guard and make sure they don't." Deepa ripped open the packet of clay. She began rolling it out on the table to warm it up.

Between them they made ten clay flowers. They stuck them all over the top layer of the cake and then stood back to admire their handiwork.

"It looks awful!" Ollie blurted out.

"Ghastly," Deepa agreed gloomily. "You know what? I guess we're going to have to be honest and own up – "

Chapter 5

They stared at each other aghast.

"I think you're right; we'd better confess," Ollie muttered. He felt so guilty. He hoped his mum and Akshay wouldn't be too upset.

"I wish I'd never written that horrible list," Deepa sighed. "Sorry, Ollie. It was meant to be a hilarious joke, but it wasn't even funny."

"We'd better go and tell someone right away," Ollie said bravely. "But who? I can't face my mum just yet."

Then they heard the steady rhythm of footsteps coming down the hall towards the kitchen. They both froze.

"Someone's coming!" Deepa whispered to Ollie in a panicky voice.

Suddenly someone opened the back door behind them. It was so unexpected, they almost jumped out of their skins. They both spun around. A pink-haired young woman in dungarees was smiling at them. She had Sausage by the collar.

"Hi, we're preparing the flower arrangements, and this dog keeps getting in our way," she said. "Can I leave him here? Thanks." She let go of Sausage's collar and shut the door without waiting for a reply. Sausage pranced across the kitchen.

Another set of footsteps coming down
the hall were getting closer. Deepa and Ollie
held their breath as someone on the other
side of the door turned the handle.

Meanwhile, Sausage could smell
the wedding cake. He jumped up on his
hindlegs and slapped his front paws onto
the table.

The table began to rock precariously, and
the cake tilted scarily.

"Sausage, no!" Ollie yelled, lunging
towards him. But he was too late.
The kitchen door opened, just as
the wedding cake crashed to the floor and
smashed into millions of pieces.

Ollie's gran stood in the doorway. She was
so shocked, she couldn't speak, as she gazed
at the remains of the cake. Deepa and Ollie
were staring at each other, horrified.

54

"Oh, Sausage, what have you done!?"
Gran exclaimed.

"Gran," Ollie began warily, but his gran held up her hand.

"Wait, Ollie, let me think." She began to pace up and down. "What a nightmare! We have to put this right before the wedding.
But how?"

Deepa glanced across at Ollie. He raised his eyebrows at her. It looked like Sausage had saved them from getting into huge trouble. But both of them felt a little guilty that the dog was getting *all* the blame.

"Right!" Gran snapped her fingers. "I've got it! I'll go and fetch your grandad, Ollie. He can clean up this mess. You two get your jackets."

"Are we going out?" Ollie asked, feeling bewildered.

"Yes," Gran said briskly. "We have four hours before I need to help your mum with her dress and veil. We're going to visit every boutique bakery in town and get all the cupcakes we can find."

"Why?" Deepa asked.

"Because I'm going to make your parents a unique new wedding cake," Gran replied. "A cupcake tower!"

Record-breaking cupcakes!

Largest cupcake ever!

This was made in the United States in 2011.

- 1,176.6 kilograms in weight

- 91.44 centimetres high

- 142.24 centimetres wide

Tallest tower of cupcakes!

This was made in India in 2019. It took around 42 hours of non-stop work to build.

- 12.69 metres high

- 18,818 cupcakes

Chapter 6

"Gran, you're a genius!" Ollie declared happily.

Gran had spent an hour driving them around the town. They'd managed to get boxes and boxes of different cupcakes. While they were out, Ollie's grandad had cleaned up the kitchen. Now they were back home, and Gran had almost finished preparing the cupcake tower. She'd stacked some pretty cake stands on top of each other, then added the cupcakes and fresh flowers from the garden.

"It looks *amazing*!" Deepa sighed.

"Look, it's nearly time for the wedding!" Gran hurried to the sink to wash her hands. "You two go and get changed. I have to help Emily get dressed. And I'll explain about the cake."

Ollie and Deepa raced upstairs, struggling to breathe.

"I feel a bit guilty that Sausage is getting *all* the blame for the spoilt cake," Deepa confided in Ollie. "Some of it *was* our fault."

"I know," Ollie replied. He looked at her. "You love Sausage, don't you?"

Deepa blushed. "Well, yes ... But I know he's *your* dog."

"Sausage can be your dog, too,"
Ollie replied kindly. Then he added.
"Especially when he's naughty!"

Deepa burst out laughing. So did Ollie.
They were still smiling when they went into
their bedrooms.

The wedding ceremony was over. All the guests had returned to the house for the wedding reception, and the bell tent was full. Ollie and Deepa were relieved to see that their parents both looked very happy. They obviously knew all about the cake, but it didn't seem to matter. Gran's cupcake tower was in pride of place on the cake table.

"Everything turned out all right in the end, didn't it?" Ollie said to Deepa. They were sitting in the sunshine eating cupcakes from Gran's wedding cake tower.

Deepa nodded. "Thanks to Sausage." She stroked the greyhound. "By the way, I haven't forgotten how you put a model of a goblin on the cake!"

Ollie laughed. "Well, what about your flower-making technique!? Those clay flowers were a totally bad idea.
And *I* haven't forgotten that you said I was charging around like an angry rhino!"

Deepa giggled. "It was a pretty good description, wasn't it?"

"Yep," Ollie admitted. "I *was* really angry."

Deepa turned to him.

"Do you think we should tell our parents the truth?" she asked. "It doesn't feel right to deceive them."

Ollie nodded. "Not today," he said, "but maybe tomorrow." He grinned. "They'll forgive us because they'll be so relieved that we're friends at last."

"Yes, we *are* friends, aren't we?" Deepa said, looking a little surprised.

She grinned at Ollie. "So, are you going to enjoy having an *older* sister, little brother?" Deepa enquired.

"I don't mind," Ollie replied. "You're the oldest, so it's down to *you* to tell Mum and Akshay what really happened to their wedding cake!"

"Thanks a lot!" Deepa huffed, and they both roared with laughter.

Ollie and Deepa at the wedding

About the author

What do you like best about writing?

I really enjoy making up stories and writing them down. What I like best about writing, though, is when other people read my stories and tell me they love them! That's very satisfying.

Narinder Dhami

Why did you want to write this book?

I love weddings, and last year I went to three of them! Every wedding is different. That's why I think a wedding is a great topic for an interesting story.

Which character do you like best and why?

I have a very soft spot for Sausage the greyhound. Years ago, a friend of mine had a rescue greyhound called Ben. Ben was lovely but he could get a little out of control, just like Sausage!

Do you have a part of the book you like best?

I love the part where Ollie sticks the goblin on the cake in place of the groom. It made me chuckle as I wrote it!

Is there anything in this book that relates to your own experiences?

Well, I am married, so yes! I enjoyed my own wedding very much. I wore a traditional red sari and gold jewellery. The only trouble is, the wedding day goes by so fast! But I have lots of lovely memories.

Have you ever been to a wedding where something went wrong?

I've never been to a wedding where the cake got smashed to bits! If anything goes wrong, it's usually because of the weather, which is something we can't control. One wedding I attended was supposed to take place in a beautiful garden under a flower arch. It rained all day, so we had to stay inside! At another wedding I went to, a storm started up when we were having photos taken outside. The bride's mother's hat blew away and landed in a tree!

What do you hope readers will get out of this book?

I hope that they'll enjoy the mix of family drama, emotion and humour.

About the illustrator

What made you want to be an illustrator?

Like most artists, I've been drawing ever since I could hold a pencil. Some of my earliest memories are of crafting greeting cards with silly doodles for friends. I also loved reading graphic novels and comics, which got me excited about drawing stories when I was growing up.

Ash Roy

What did you like best about illustrating this book?

I loved illustrating the scenes with Sausage. He's sweet. The commotion of him toppling the cake is brilliant!

Which character do you like best and why?

I think I liked Ollie best because I really enjoyed illustrating his range of emotions. He goes from being sad then angry to utter panic through the story.

How long does it take to draw each illustration?

Smaller illustrations take me around 2–4 hours, and bigger ones take around 6–10 hours.

What was the most difficult thing about illustrating this book?

The most challenging thing about illustrating this book was narrowing down the details in a scene, especially the ones that show the wedding celebrations. I wanted to show all the decorations and guests mingling without it looking too busy.

How do you bring a character to life in an illustration?

I use my sketchbook for the initial sketches. I can play around and try different versions of a scene to see what works best. Ollie and Deepa shared so many activities that the more I worked on them, the better I could capture their personalities.

Have you ever been to a wedding where something went wrong?

I haven't ever been to a wedding where something went wrong, but I'm guessing it might not be as amusing a as in this story.

What would you add to the top of the cake if you had a choice?

I have several models of birds; perhaps a tiny owl could accompany the goblin and the bride.

Book chat

Have you ever been to a wedding? What was it like?

What skills and solutions did Deepa and Ollie each bring to the disaster?

Do you think any of the characters changed from the start of the book to the end? How?

What did you think of Gran's plan to make a new wedding cake?

Did you think Deepa and Ollie should have told the truth? Why, or why not?

If you were in Deepa and Ollie's position, what would you have done?

If you could ask the author or illustrator a question, what would you ask?

Does this book remind you of any other stories you know? How?

What did you think of the book at the start? Did you change your mind as you read it?

Book challenge:
Design your own unique wedding cake.

Collins
BIG CAT

Published by Collins
An imprint of HarperCollins*Publishers*

The News Building
1 London Bridge Street
London SE1 9GF
UK

Macken House
39/40 Mayor Street Upper
Dublin 1
D01 C9W8
Ireland

Author: Narinder Dhami
Illustrator: Ash Roy (Astound Illustration Agency)
Publisher: Laura White
Product manager: Caroline Green
Series editor: Charlotte Raby
Development editor: Catherine Baker
Commissioning editor: Suzannah Ditchburn
Project manager: Emily Hooton
Copyeditor: Sally Byford
Proofreader: Catherine Dakin
Cover designer: Sarah Finan
Typesetter: 2Hoots Publishing Services Ltd
Production controller: Katharine Willard

Printed in the UK.

MIX
Paper | Supporting
responsible forestry
FSC
www.fsc.org
FSC™ C007454

This book is produced from independently certified FSC™
paper to ensure responsible forest management.

For more information visit: www.harpercollins.co.uk/green

Made with responsibly sourced
paper and vegetable ink

Scan to see how we are reducing
our environmental impact.

Download the teaching notes and
word cards to accompany this book at:
http://littlewandle.org.uk/signupfluency/

Get the latest Collins Big Cat news at
collins.co.uk/collinsbigcat